Impatiently Inpatient

Hailey Sprandel

Presentation by *BookLeaf Publishing*

Web: www.bookleafpub.com

E-mail: info@bookleafpub.com

ISBN: 9789357442183

First edition 2023

To Adam, who pushed me in ways I can't explain to keep going and to fight even when it doesn't feel worth fighting for. To all of Oaklawn staff, Summit Pointe staff, and 988, thank you for all of your support and help keeping me alive. To Cloud, who was with me from poem one to the end and is always encouraging towards my mental health. And to Jessie, who has also pushed me in many ways to seek help in places that I was too scared to on my own. Thank you for infinity.

PREFACE

This collection of poems were created during and after two inpatient stays in October through January. Reader discretion is advised as these poems contain very difficult topics. They follow my growth and mindset while and after being suicidal. I hope everyone can connect with and experience change like I have even if you're not out of the thick of it.

Day One

I sleep, yet still tired
If I weep, I'm a liar
Sinks into my skin
Sets me in fire
My situation: dire
Used to inspire
But now, always tired

"How're you?"
"I'm fine"
Wasting away the time
Watching days go by
Where I suffer, still alive
No longer to thrive
And barely able to survive
Locked in
My mind
Wish it was thoughtless
Sometimes
Don't mean to whine
But sure, I'm doing fine

Agitation is a danger
Unsafe in anger
The anguish that lingers

Diminished and simmers
Deep down it coagulates
Grates, stains, and agitates
I'm afraid
It's so hard to live when distain weighs thickly
coated in pain

Things can never be the same
No matter how hard I try
In vain
If someone could cauterize my brain
Stop the bleeding of feelings that I have no hope
in dealing with
Stealing any wish I have of a future
I'm left reeling, unfeeling
Yet keeling over in disproportionate emotions
Like oceans
Unyielding
Pull under, drown you, full of thunder
Slam your feeble body against boulders
Doesn't make you bolder
Makes you colder, smolder
And makes you wonder
Why aren't I six feet under?

These thought plunder and plague me on a daily
basis
No oasis is safest when I'm in the spaces
Faithless

Heart races and shakes
And faces I can't remember the names of
Never be good enough
Therefore
I'm done

Crying Girls

Crying echos off walks and through doors and
down halls
I do what i can even if it's not much
I move slow, speak, quiet, don't touch
My hands, brush the floor as I get low in my
arms feel sore
I don't know what's in store and I'm fearful
Looking at the tearful girl in front of me
She must feel lonely, ran by somebody else
And in her, I see myself
I speak of deep, shallow, and trivial flings to get
her mind off of things
Then she asks me to leave
I rise in seat back to the commons
Not uncommon to face rejection in my head, I
mention
As I said, she's slinks out and grab paper and sits
down
With a frown she and I begin to write in
comfortable silence
It's quiet, but I don't mind it because I got her to
stop crying
I'd be lying to say there's no time for tears
But it hurts me deep down
Piercing my heart and ears

I do for others what I can't do for myself
It might not be the best, but at least I feel better
if I can help
Maybe that's selfish but I hate others feeling
helpless
So then maybe it's selfless
I don't know, I just guess

Impatiently Inpatient

Cold rooms to make tempers simmer
White hues to make panic thinner
Bunches of pills to dilute your innards
Do you feel like a winner?
Stuck, trapped inside, numbly swallowing
dinner?
Choking, slowing, and agitation growing
Felling like throwing, up or throwing fists with
People who always bitch
About how unfair, unheard, and unhappy they
are
I sit in silence, littered with scars
I watch stars in quiet late nights
We're overwhelmed with the same fights
But damn, I'd father fight you
You're rude, disrespectful, and have a disgusting
attitude
You make me want to bash your head in every
time you scream about how you're "going to
sue"
Slamming doors, threatening, and hollar
Your "fucking phone" you don't deserve
You're a stupid toddler
I lose all respect for you as your volume grows
louder

Your tension that echos through halls
Makes situations a downer
I cower against walls because I'm trying so
fucking hard not to start
You don't realize, all of us want out of the dark
I sit in my car, midnight at the park
Blood and anguish leak in waves during my
drunken stupor haze
You make me wish I would've stayed

Your piercing voice hits like static noise on the
loudest setting
No getting away
No choice but to sit, listen and stay
I just want a fucking break

Highly Educated

I know I'm not a nurse
But this must be your first
Patient your treating, you see
Because I'm lacking empathy and patience in
how you're treating me
You must believe I'm in need
But I receive nothing
It's something, you can't give
I think you'd be more productive in a different
career
Since the words you speak shrewd my heart and
ears
I can't bear to hear your discrimination
That must have an inflation on your ego
The more "triggered" you are
The bigger I feel the impulse to make my scars
Because they're apart of me
I can't take them back, on skin they have to be
Why don't you see
How uncomfortable, undesirable a situation
you're making
Should I live my life in fear and concern in how
others view?
Lie broken, wrapped in bandages?
What do you want me to do?!

It's my body I can't change so please give me a
clue
Why I'm such an ugly monster, a "trigger", or a
statistic to you
These wounds aren't really new, no blood yet
this huge concern you construe
No one has said anything in the thirty minutes
that elude
Yet your determined to make me feel unwanted,
invalid, and used
So thanks and screw you

What Are You?

Are you internally idle? Or feeling like a tidal?
Constantly suicidal?
Let us take your vitals
A couple pills to wash it down?
Don't wear a frown
"Your a queen" so wear a crown

How's Your mood?

Today I am a one
I don't sit at the window in the sun
I sleep and dream of pointless things
And nightmares sing me away
Today I have no future
I sit and wallow thinking of sutures that pierced
my skin because monsters win
And the walls that make me stay

Want To Play A Game?

Shaking violently, sitting silently, quietly
Brewing and stewing, and thoughts of misusing
The story's the same but always eluding
Confusing, this is war
Abusing, thoughts hitting the walls
I'm losing, inside my head
Subduing, everything I work so hard for
It's a crime to be fine and you'll always get
maximum sentence
The judge will always be the worst, because it's
you cursed internal critic
How do you live with it?
I'm sick of it
Always juggling on a sixty story building
It's killing and chilling, air is freezing
Can you feel your heart beating?
Out of your chest, so restless
"Are the meds working?"
"What's your moods?"
"How're you?"
What's the use, I'll just recluse
They try to change but the ending always stays
the same
I'm tired of being a pawn in this continuous
game

Like I said I'm sick of it
So I'd rather forfeit

Trigger Warning

They say to change the darkness you have to
turn the lights on
But it's too fucking white, like staring at the
bright sun
I'm blinded I can't see
I'm reminded in the darkness creeps back on me
Can't breathe, suffocating
It's integrating in my head
Sedating without my consent
Did I need to be more verbal?
I thought no and stop where enough?
Should I have been more physical?
Maybe but he liked it rough
So into my brain, I seat, swim in my mentality
Always show over emotionally
Why does it keep coming back, why the fuck is
this happening?
It's excruciating, elevating, my anxiety,
retaliating
I hate this, I wish things were different
Instead, I'm forced to live in relive in it
To feel his skin, touching mine in to act like I'm
just fine
To let him in my house, because I'm just too
damn kind
Praying that the stars couldn't line to end it

End this stupid, fucking note, and my life, and
this feeling of his dick htoting the back of my
throat
End my fist slamming against his chest weakly
End my suffering, and give me a rest completely
End my being of eternally being upset
Make me forget, him being erect
His hands crawling, his complacent tone
The way his voice sounds over the phone
Parents say I should've known better
I guess seventeen makes it your fault whether
you wanted it or not
Forget his fucking child in which I gave it all up
for
And the fact that I opened up a stupid fucking
closed door
I was just a kid how was I to know?
Still having a lot of innocence because you
sheltered
So under heat and conflict I swelter
I break under the pressure and forget everything
I'm supposed to remember
Why is it always my fault?!
Why does a red light mean go?
What is a stop, a please don't, a no?
I thought I was Allowed to change my mind?
I only agreed under your pressure at the time
anyways

I recoil for an ending days, for the past stays the
same, and I'm unable to read it from my rotting
brain
I was just a kid you were in your thirties
My boyfriends brother, shouldn't you have
known better?
So I'm cursed forever, and yet I endeavored
asking for it three times I guess
November first, November fourth and the first
time, October tenth
I always opened the door, for one reason or
another
I never told a fucking soul for months, I lied for
you
Now I'm just a number
A little statistic to be scratched away and
forgotten
But I can never forget
That luxury is never often
I'm locked in, sobbing my soul into this book
Hoping somehow it can get back what you took
But instead, I'm left forever be shook, like a
snow globe, slammed up and down and all
around, unable to know where to look
So I sit instead with a frowned, i lay in
cascading darkness that vignettes my vision,
always wishing that I could turn the worlds
noise down
Silence the sounds of alarms in my head
And forget

Get To The Point

What's the point of living?
What's the point of not giving, into desires that
are winning?
That start fires within me?
Always singing in binging on bad things that are
sending my lifeline
Lately things don't shine as bright, my site is
muted, and I've concluded it's always to do with
bad intentions
My mind mentions daily: "Hailey! Don't you
want to slit your wrists?!"
" don't you want to satiate that craving that you
miss?"
" don't you want to give death? Just a little kiss?
I insist it'll clear you if you witness."
" just a little deeper this time, isn't it fun dancing
line?"
It's an endless ballroom with no intention to stop
anytime soon, the music is out of tune, and
everyone dancing are pictures of the past
The thing about dead bodies is that they never
last
And the last thing you remember, is there
dismembered image like a cold December, air

frigid you're inside, so livid you barely feel the
frost
So you stay lost, ever enchanted in the
overpowering dance
You only have so many chances to dance
frantically to escape, with two left feet you glide
towards the date of expiration
Hasten, your steps, for you never know how
many shoe drops you have left
On the ground now, the bodies dance feverishly
into your chest
"why are you depressed?" they sitting quietly
"why are you filled with constant anxiety?" they
asked breathlessly
I don't know anymore, and I returned with the
mess filled life that breathes out of me

Do You Hear It?

My screams baby can you hear it?
Do you listen to every fear soaked lyric?
Does it hurt you when you get near it?
Your insides, does it sheer it?
The blood dripping, leaving a stain
The slight throb spilling out of my veins
The calm from me that's overcame
I don't know how else to explain
Wrapping it up
Soothing the pain
Numbing the ache
Fire in my brain
Am I insane?
Do you see the beetles attacking my membrane?

The Wrong Choice

It should be my choice
To take my life
To leave this strife
Under the blade of a knife
It should be my decision
Just to stop living
My heart's not in it
Think my lifelines thinning
I should have an option
Do you no longer be locked in?
To make it all stop
I definitely didn't opt in
I don't want to wake up
Slather on make up
And go through the day
Waiting for life to shake up

Are You Sure?

Cast all your anxieties on him
Because he can handle it?
Can he manage it, when you're staggering
Dragging your feet, everlasting
Can he pass it? Move past it?
While you're slandering
Your floundering is too distracting
Cast on him be cast out
Is that how this works?
Are you sure?
That last outburst won't turned him away?
Today's exile will make him stay
Are you sure? Is it worth it?
Are you worthy?
Can you force him to carry your hurting?
This deeply in raged fire that's burning?
You cast your anxieties
Yet throw out your sobriety
You suck down your prescriptions
But that doesn't sound like surviving to me

Burgundy Webs

Burgundy Webs draw pathways and line my relationships and dance with me at parties. They dance over skin of the spider that made them. Aren't they beautiful? Everyone screams in horror and the web drips to the ground growing longer. The spider goes home to spin webs as that's all she's ever known. She tore more material and spun the night away. The next day, someone asked her "Why don't you fly instead little spider?" She said it's not the same. "Plus I'm a spider I'm only meant to make webs." So home she went to delicately hand spin and to cover her self in burgundy webs that shined in the Moonlight. People hate her and her webs and for some reason they don't understand. It feels like she's been cut through by hot knife, she she goes home alone, and bandages herself in the sticky burgundy webs. She cries, it never helps, and no one can appreciate her webs like she does. How far she's come to make them. One day, the spider looks in the mirror. Pure terror on her face, and she realizes she was a butterfly all along. Not meant to be covered in the horribly suffocating webs and her wings, tattered with holes for she had been using them as material for

a burgundy webs. Too late now, she's unable to
fly. So she goes home and does only what she
knows. She spins her burgundy webs and cradles
herself in them to sleep.

Poor Puppy

I imagine me, laying in the snow
Clothes, soaked from the cold
The ground is stained rose
The bottle, no longer full
Fingers froze around the neck
Cries for help no longer echo
Saying I want to be better is a stretch
When my actions say I want to let go instead
If I really wanted to live, I'd try harder
The same could be said if I wanted to die though
So I get neither and waste in limbo
You'd think after so long I'd be smarter
I'd know what I want and how to get there
But lately I find it hard to find the will to care
Sorry, I tend to overshare
I know it isn't fair
What about me?
I think selfishly
I sit, staring
Always helplessly
Will someone help the sad puppy?
It's been kicked around too much
Beaten, starved, and left in the dust
All it's learned is how not to trust
It's like that's all it does now

So quiet, silent puppy, you never speak aloud
No tricks, silly puppy? Wow, your parents must
be proud.
Can't find home, stupid puppy? You're always
lost in the crowd
Why do you frown, little puppy nobody? Oh,
that's right, no one wants you around.
You'd be better off in the ground
Dig yourself a hole, pathetic puppy, seems it's
all your worth
Stop speaking, disgusting puppy, you're mangy
covered in all that dirt
Just do it, you suicidal puppy, for someone who
follows others all the time
You worthless, poor puppy, directions you don't
know how to mind
I guess lost puppies can't do anything right
All bark, no bite
The pitiful pound puppies, they always give up
on the fight
So go away, deserted puppy, it's all you've left
to do
Don't worry, unwanted puppy, because no one's
worried about you

Are You Lying?

I'm the common denominator
Been dealing with pain for so long
It's been up for the taking
So why does everyone scream I'm wrong
Why do words yell I'm faking
I must be exaggerating
If I'm still waking at days breaking
Can't be hating myself that much
Only just a touch
How would you rate your pain
Ten being the worst and zero being none
I swear I'm not having fun
To my head, holding a gun, shaking
Tell me I'm fucking dreaming
God, what I would give for it to be a lie
Obviously, it must be if I'm still alive
I just want quiet, I want silence
But in those times is the worst of internal
violence
I wish I could stop
I'm fine because I'm not bleeding
Well, give me a minute, and that fact will be
fleeting
Believe me or go leaving

Same Old

Why do my words always sound the same?
What do I really gain from the pain?
What doesn't kill you makes you stronger
I think it just means you struggle a little longer
Tell me ", Father, what's the point
Skills. A fake that I quote have "
The knowledge that things "can only get so bad?
"

Then give me the faCts
11 minutes and someone doesn't get their life
back
1.2 million lost from their mental attack.
Where is ugly, but what about the fight inside?
The fight to survive yourself?
Have you felt the past few days?
Have you reached out? Asked for help?
Have you dealt with out if you believe there's no
end?
The agony always depends
Talk to friends? Don't you'll just burden
They're hurting will worsen
How could you take away my only daughter?
I'm sorry to be such a bother
Could you solder my mental injuries?
Insecurities?

Save me from an eternity?
Always suffering

How Do I Pray?

Cake, balloons, good tunes , prayer
Everyone's excited, the whole town's invited
Fear, despair, sobriety
Damage, ravage, anxiety
God, where are you?
Brokenness, messy, lives, failures
"Praise God, amen! "Hello again
What can I say that hasn't already been said?
Why do I have to pray
In the same way
Every fucking Sunday
Where is my worthy?
I can barely worship
What does it mean anymore?
What am I praying for?
If I never ask for anything
How does nothing speak to a king?
Instead, I sent freezing
I needing, wanting freeing
But trying believing
Is it a feeling?
Great master, unyielding
How do I speak?
I suppose I'm too meek
Prayer is what I sick today, Lord

Have mercy
I guess, help me not be
Depressed
Am I asking too much?
How do I know?
How about this am I supposed to go?
I sit down, closed my eyes, bow my head
Putting on a show
My worth in prayer is about how far I can throw
And damn, I can't toss far
So please, show me where you are
Cracking bones against
Stones that aren't mine to be thrown
I'm supposed to know, have faith
Read my Bible so I can relate
To all these friendly strangers
When all I feel is danger
How am I supposed to keep my anger of myself
away?
Please shape me, save me
Stop my suffering of another day
Fuck I don't know the right things to say
To you, to them, to me
I barely sleep, eat, and breathe
So please tell me, help me
What do I pray for?

Is It Worth It?

Memories shoot through dark hallways and run
always run down dark pathways and endings of
mazes creep up in the corners
Feeling trapped, caged, and laced
Power is zapped and ravings enraged
Don't know the path I guess the one less
traveled by
Leaving the past, we don't see eye to eye
I don't want it to last
Don't want to want to die
But my minds fried
And I've cried way too many times to count
Every ounce of my energy leaves in waves
I wish it would stay
Every day is a new day
But living in a haze makes it worthless
Is it worth it?
I guess if it's temporary

Taking Charge

Birds chitter, used to be enjoyable
Birds staying, techniques aren't deployable
I'm evading, the invasion on my skin
From the monsters that are chasing
Cause my heart racing
Why am I always facing?
They're casing and staking out my weaknesses
I though I was better than this
Im shaking
So hard to handle
Nothing holds a candle to the scan or that
channels inside
Makes me cry and fries my organs, shreds my
mind
A tiny amount
But all the time
Im ready to be better
Im ready to weather the weather that makes me
wetter whether or not I want it to
I'm stronger than you know
More intelligent than you think
And more important that you could ever imagine
You can't stand it
I may not face Goliath but I have my own giants

Im kicking ass, taking names, and standing here
defiant
You're challenge is nothing
Im ready to fight for something
And damn now I have something to fight for
You won't know what's happening
I'll score before you know what's in store
I feel it in my core
I'm filled with confidence and lost in it
And your despondence makes me laugh
For I pity you now
Not the other way around
Sit and sulk and I'll relish while I finally make
ground

Two Sides To Every Coin

Back again, how many times before I learn
All these emotions I can't discern
My hearts on fire, frontal cortex gorged out
Brain desires to die more times than I can count
Why does it hound me every second of every
day?
What can I do to get the pain to go away?
Liver put through a tenderizer, lungs put on a
flame
Cook them medium rare they ask, I'm always
the one to blame
Eviscerate what's left of my soul and carve away
at it to
Destroying every little piece of me whatever
benefits you
But damn what I want to say it's a fuck you is
due
Give my shit back, and I'll hold it, renewed
I say it's my turn to be happy
That's something that can't be construed
You've pissed me off now you better step back
for a few
I am deserving
I am worth it
I am worthy

I'm perfect
I'm lovely and crafty and uniquely gorgeous
I'm loving myself one day at a time
Just hear me bellow my chorus
You should forfeit, for I am for it
And there's no ignoring my life is no longer
thinning
For I am winning

A Sinky Inky Feeling

I stand flatly in blue ink stained clothing
Certainly not happy, but definitely full of
loathing
Everyone stoking, this fire inside me
There's no hiding from where this monsters
residing
I'm starving, slowly carving away at my insides
I can't make you understand
No matter how hard I try, I can't
My world is gray and yours is a black and white
slant
Dropping drippings of blotchy colorlessness
They mixed together in my head to make up my
hopelessness
I'm sorry I've even spoken, a token of how I feel
Because all you ever do is invalidate, making it
less real
This inky stained world is bitter
Talk of success over failure
If I'm barely breathing is stealing and making
me reeling unfeeling
Your misleading and lying and now I'm sobbing
and crying but you know what?
I don't give a fuck
I don't need your validation, that ship has sailed

And if my progression isn't good enough, it
doesn't mean I failed
Screw you, for your idiotic train is derailed
How about you look at my middle finger in use
that for scale
There's no fun with you, no sun with you, no
one's won with you
So I'm done with you